How to Build a Ventriloquist Dummy

A Step by Step Guide for the Home Carpenter

How to
Build a Dummy

You can't spend all your time sitting in front of the mirror practicing voice and lip control. When you're not, you can be putting thought and work into this little partner of yours who will one day be the mainstay of your ventriloquist act.

You see, you yourself are only half the act. Having the voice and nothing more doesn't make you a ventriloquist, as you know him today. If you remember I explained earlier that ventriloquism is only an illusion; that it's the art of using our keen sense of sight to deceive our often inaccurate sense of hearing. To do that we must have the voice of the ventriloquist (which is heard by our ears) and the moving dummy or object (which is seen by our eyes). You can't have ventriloquism with only the voice or only the object. You must have both to complete the illusion we call ventriloquism.

In other words, when you have obtained the voice, you still need the other half. You need the lips, other than your own, which will move at the same time with the words you create ventriloquially. In short, you now need a dummy. Where do you get one? Well, you could go out and buy a dummy in a toy or department store or a magic shop. You might even find an old one in a pawn shop or secondhand store. Either way, you'd have a dummy you could use. But it might be more fun, and less expensive, for you to build your own. Not only that, but if you make it yourself, it can be whatever kind of a dummy you'd like. It can be a boy or a girl. It can have a turned up nose or a lump on the head. It can be curly and blonde or have a red headed crew cut. Whereas, the dummy you buy will have to remain pretty much as it was when you got it. Furthermore, I believe that if you build your own dummy you'll have a greater feeling of pride and accomplishment. And I'm sure you'll also have a certain unexplainable attachment and kinship with the dummy because you created it. It's part of you, your imagination and your talents.

There is one exception to what I have just said. That was a dummy I once tried to build in Cleveland. I was touring with the Major Bowes

Amateurs at the time. One night at the theatre somebody in the troupe who was hanging around my dressing room said to me, "Winchell, you've only got one dummy. What would you do if something happened to him? Suppose he got lost or stolen, or suppose there was a fire? You'd be out of luck!"

For some reason I had never thought about this, but from that moment on I did. I kept thinking about it until finally I got scared. The fellow was right. If anything did happen to Jerry I couldn't go on . . . I'd have no act . . . I'd be out of a job. So I decided right after the matinee I'd go back to the hotel and make another dummy of Jerry.

I left the theatre and went straight to the nearest hardware store and bought all the supplies I needed, and headed for the hotel. In those days the Bowes Amateur Units were so famous and popular wherever they went, that they were always asked to stay at the swankiest hotel at a very low rate. Cleveland was no exception. I had a beautiful corner room with a tile bath which contained a big comfortable bathtub.

I walked into the plush lobby, loaded down with my bags of plaster, clay, paint, brushes, and a few assorted pots and pans. I looked like I had at least come to remodel the place if not, in fact, to tear it down. People stared at me as I rode the elevator up to my room. Then the fun began!

You see, my idea was this. With the clay I'd

sculpture a head to look like Jerry's and then cover it with plaster. What the plaster hardened I'd take it off the clay and have a hard shell of Jerry's head. I'd put papier mâché into the shell and, when it in turn hardened, I'd knock off the plaster shell and have a new second head of Jerry.

So, I started. I sculptured a pretty good likeness of Jerry's head out of the clay. Then I mixed up some plaster in one of the pots. The question now was where to do the actual work. I was sure the hotel wouldn't condone even a Bowes Amateur covering the deep pile of their carpets with a coating of plaster, clay and paint. There was only one place—the bathtub! I put the clay head in the bottom of the tub and was all ready to pour on the plaster. But something was missing. The right way to do it is to put the clay head in a deep wooden box and simply pour in the wet plaster until the clay is covered. This keeps the plaster from spreading all over everything. But I didn't have any wooden box. So I did the next best thing. I manufactured four sides out of the cardboard the laundry had sent back in my shirts and joined the corners with some strips of Scotch tape. It didn't have a bottom except the bottom of the bathtub.

I started to pour in the plaster. As fast as I poured it in, it escaped out of the corners of the cardboard. I kept pouring it in, and it kept oozing out. I used up all the plaster I had made and still it wasn't enough to cover the clay head. So I rushed back into the bedroom and made up another batch of plaster. I poured this into the cardboard frame; it oozed out into the tub too. I made some more and finally got the clay head submerged in plaster. But, by a strange coincidence, the tub was also deep in soggy plaster. Plaster which was hardening by the second. At the same moment my watch showed that it was time for me to be at the theatre. So I dashed out of the hotel hoping nobody would discover the mess in my bathtub.

When I returned later that night after the show my plaster had hardened beautifully. It had also hardened everyplace else. My bathtub was half filled with rock-hard plaster with the clay head somewhere in the middle of it. What was I going to do? How was I going to get the plaster out? The only tool I had was a penknife, but I went to work. This was like trying to carve faces into Mt. Rushmore with a hairpin. Now I was scared stiff! Wait till the hotel found out!

After a restless night's sleep I got up and rushed back to the hardware store again for a hammer and chisel. I hammered and chiselled at the bathtub. This made racket enough to disturb the other guests, but it didn't disturb the plaster in my bathtub. It wouldn't come loose. It was stuck, but good. Now I was really in a panic! And it was time to go to the theatre for the matinee. I went leaving a "Please Do Not Disturb" sign hanging on my door.

Immediately after the matinee I dashed back to the hotel hoping I could chip a little plaster out of the tub. I didn't get any farther than the lobby. The manager was waiting for me. "Winchell," he roared, "what are you doing up there in that bathtub?"

"I'll get it out," I said with a weak laugh.

"You'll get out!" he replied sharply. "And right now! That crazy plaster has clogged up the hotel plumbing!!!!"

He handed me my bill. There, among a 25¢ charge for a phone call and 65¢ for a breakfast, was a little item—1 bathtub—$25.00. Needless to say I paid it and departed. Proving, I guess, that sometimes two heads are not better than one.

In the intervening years I've been a guest of that same hotel in Cleveland many times. The moment I walk in, the manager starts kidding me. He shakes my hand, and says, "Winchell, come on down in the basement. I want to show you something. We've got a bathtub down there half filled with plaster."

I suggested that you start building your dummy at the same time as you're developing your ventriloquial voice. In this way, when you are ready to use the dummy, it will be ready for you.

Having decided to build a dummy, you probably will say to yourself, "How do I go about it?" Well, the old saying that there are more ways than one to "skin a cat," holds true with making a dummy. So I'll explain several different ways of how you can make one.

From the beginning of time, most of the dummies, puppets, and marionettes have been, for the most part, made out of wood. You may ask why did they use wood instead of some other material. Couldn't they have made dummies out of stone or cement or marble. They could have, but wood was the natural choice for many obvious reasons. For one thing wood is lighter than stone, which is a help to the ventriloquist who has to hold and manipulate the dummy. Also, the head and face have to be carved and sculptured to look as life-like as possible, and wood is much easier material to carve than stone. So, years ago, when they didn't have all the modern tools and machines that we have today, they carved the dummies out of wood. There may be in existence some freak dummies carved out of some kind of stone, but I've never seen one. Of course there are the stone idols the Ancients used, but I'm talking about dummies that are animated and manipulated by a ventriloquist.

While through the years most dummies have been made of wood, they could be made out of other materials as well. You can make one out of papier mâché, and with the proper tools and know-how, you could probably make one from today's new plastics.

However, since this is probably the first dummy you've ever made, and because you probably want to use it as quickly as possible, I'll first explain what I think is the easiest and quickest way for you to build one. This will be made out of papier mâché. Later I'll describe how you can make one out of wood. Let me say right here that no matter what material you make the dummy out of, the construction and installation of the moving parts such as the mouth is the same for all.

The important part of the ventriloquist's dummy is naturally the head. All the mechanism for controlling the moving parts is mounted inside the head and on the pole. This is the part that creates the illusion for the audience. The body of the dummy is relatively unimportant except for the costume which will be discussed in a future chapter. So, in building your dummy you start with the head. And in this case you're going to make the head out of papier mâché.

Before you start to work, be sure you have all the tools and materials needed to construct the dummy. You don't want to get to a certain point and have to stop because you don't have some little nail or a paint brush. Here is a list of what you'll need. Get these and then I'll explain how and when you use each of them.

MATERIAL

1) A piece of round broom or mop handle about 18 inches long.

2) Five to ten pounds of non-hardening clay (Plastaline or Plastacine.)
3) Two rolls of good thick paper towels. Each roll of a different color.
4) A half pound package of paperhanger's paste.
5) 1 pound plastic wood.

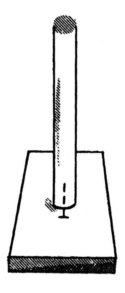

Fig. 2—Start off by nailing pole to a wooden base.

When you have the necessary material, you are ready to begin. The most important part of the dummy's head is the face. In real life it's our face that people look at, and it's from the face that people get a partial idea of our character. The same holds true with the dummy. Is he cute, dopey, sad or tough?

Therefore, before you begin to construct the face you must have some thoughts in mind as to what kind of person you want your dummy to be. Once having decided what kind of a dummy you desire, the next step is for you to proceed to sculpture him with features which will partly disclose his character.

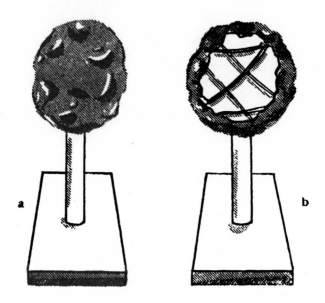

a   b

Fig. 3-a—Pack a solid mass of clay ten inches high, on upper half of pole.
Fig. 3-b—Alternate method of packing clay around ball of newspaper.

In making a papier-mâché head you must first make a head out of clay. First take the pole, that 18 inch piece of mop handle, and nail it to a strong piece of board. This is to keep it from falling over while you are working with it

(Fig. 2). Next put on the pole a mass of clay approximately the size you wish the head to be (Fig. 3-a). If you can't manage to get that much clay you can roll up a ball of newspaper and put a thick layer of clay completely around it (Fig. 3-b). Make your ball of newspaper on the pole and tie it with string or Scotch tape to hold it together while putting the clay on it.

Fig. 4—Begin sculpturing the head.

Remember, too, when you're shaping a head of clay that you must also make a neck for the dummy. So put clay down on the pole in a rounded fashion for the neck. The thickness of the neck will be determined by the size of the head. A dummy's neck is thin like a little boy's. And one more thing—*be sure the neck is rounded on the bottom,* as indicated in the illustration (Fig. 4).

Now you have a round faceless head and neck on the pole. Your next step is to mold a face. What the face will be like is entirely in your hands. Some faces will be better than others depending upon your individual talent and ability. But to start modeling the face push the clay in a little for the eyes and build it up a little for the cheeks and more so for the nose and ears. You might try creating the features by putting on little pieces of clay and when they've taken the shape you desire smooth them over with your fingers. This is the way all sculptors work.

Here's another little money-saving trick. When you are molding the head, sculpture the hair right on it, too. This can be painted later and save you the expense of buying a wig for your dummy. Just shape the top and back of the head in the style of hair-do you want your dummy to have. It can be wavy, or parted or even in a crew cut (Fig. 5).

There is one important point to remember in molding the face in the clay. The areas where you depress the clay such as the eyes, between the lips, nostrils, under the chin, must be slightly exaggerated or enlarged. This is because you're later going to put on layers of papier mâché, and each layer takes away some of the definition of the features

At this point, you have a completed head of clay. Now you are ready to apply what is known as papier mâché. With the papier mâché you're going to make a shell, an empty head, that looks exactly like the clay head. The dummy's head has to be a hollow shell because there must be room inside to install the mechanism for the moving parts.

Fig. 5—The clay model in the finishing stages. (Molded with and without hair.)

Making papier mâché is very easy. On the list of needed material was two rolls of paper towel, each of a different color. Tear those towels one color at a time into pieces and strips of from one inch to two inches in size, and then tear a lot of smaller pieces too. Be sure that you tear the towels rather than cut them with a scissors. Scissors will give the pieces a sharp defined edge, whereas tearing them gives each piece a frayed ragged edge which is what you want in making papier mâché. After you have torn the paper towel, the next thing is to soak all the pieces in water. Don't mix the pieces of the different colored towel together. Keep each color separate. You will only use one color at a time.

While the pieces of paper towel are soaking, mix up a small bowl full of the paperhanger's paste. You'll find the directions on the bag which you buy at the hardware store. At the same time get out your small stiff paint brush. When the pieces of towel have been thoroughly soaked in the water, take out one piece at a time, shake the excess water off and place it on the clay head. Then with the brush cover the first piece with the paste. Don't be skimpy with the paste. Remember it's the paste as well as the paper that makes the papier mâché. Then put on a second piece of towel, and be sure that it over-laps a little on the first piece. Coat it generously with paste. Continue to put on these overlapping pieces of towel and smearing them with paste, until you have covered the entire head with one layer (Fig. 6). Use the larger pieces for broad areas such as the forehead, cheeks, and the top and back of the head and the neck. And use the very small pieces for the fine delicate work around the mouth, nose, eyes and ears.

Fig. 6—Apply the first layer of paper.

Once you have applied one layer of paper to the clay head it is not necessary to allow it to dry before putting on the second layer or the third or the fourth. Just put one layer on top of another. You don't have to put on all the layers at the same time. You can put one layer on one day and another the next without hurting your work. The only "must" being that you must change color of paper for each new layer. This is done to make sure that you completely cover the head each time. If, for instance, you put a layer of white over a layer of white you wouldn't be able to tell whether your second layer had completely covered the first. When the pieces of paper towel are wet and covered with paste they all look pretty much alike. So by using a different color for each layer you can tell that you've entirely covered the head when the first layer no longer shows through.

If you put on about six layers of paper, alternating with a different color each time, you'll find that it will make a nice hard shell. Don't forget when putting on the paper to be sure to cover the neck, and also put some down on the pole itself. When you have put on all the required layers of toweling you will have a wet papier mâché head. So, right here let's call "signals off" and re-check the important points: (1) tear the paper towels, don't cut them with a scissors, (2) use the paste generously, (3) be sure the pieces overlap, (4) alternate the colors.

Once you have put on the several layers of paper, there's nothing you can do but wait till it dries. This may take several days depending on your climate and weather. Feel it every eight or ten hours. As long as it feels a little damp, it is not thoroughly dry. You must wait until it is bone dry before you can do any more work on it (Fig. 7). So don't be impatient. Even if it takes an extra day for it to dry all the way through, wait! Otherwise you may find that you'll have to do the entire job over again. When it has finally dried, however, you will have a good strong, stiff papier mâché head that will last for a long time. Your work now depends on which way you made your clay head. If you sculptured the head

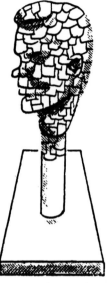

Fig. 7—After six layers let the papier mâché become bone dry.

from a solid mass of clay or used the idea of the ball of newspaper inside the clay, your job now is to get the clay out of the hard papier mâché shell around it. The way to do this is to cut the head into two halves (Fig. 8). The one half with the face and neck and the other half with the back of the head. Now take a sharp kitchen knife and cut the head in two halves. This leaves the ears on the back half of the head.

After sawing you then have two papier mâché halves filled with clay. Don't expect the clay to

come out in one large hunk. It won't. You'll
have to pick the clay out in small pieces with
your fingers or some tool. Let me warn you to

Fig. 8—Cut head apart as shown.

take your time. Don't try to hurry it by pulling
out big chunks of clay. If you are careless or
hurried in removing it you might rip off part of
the nose or mouth. After you get the clay out
then coat the inside of the head with shellac. As
I've said previously, take it easy. Do the work
slowly and you'll do it right. If it's done right
you'll then be ready to install the moving parts.
Like Gepetto's Pinocchio your dummy is on its
way to coming to life.

Quite often you have heard the ventriloquist refer to his dummy as you "little wooden head." The obvious reason for this is that the head is made of wood. In the first part of this chapter, I described how to make the papier mâché head because it can be made easily and quickly. Some of you, however, may wish to start out with a head of wood, just as those of you who begin with papier mâché may later want to switch to a wooden head after you've learned the tricks and techniques of manipulation. So with a few more illustrations I'll explain how you can make a "little wooden head."

It may look as though all you have to do is take a block of wood, a knife, and start to work carving out a dummy's head. That's what you do all right, but it isn't quite as simple as it sounds. A lot more planning, sculpturing, and honest sweat has to go into the making of the wooden head than went into the one of papier mâché. I'm not trying to discourage you from working in wood. I just want you to know ahead of time what you're getting into. On the other hand it will be fun, and you'll learn how to use some new tools and material, so I'll get down to describing how you go about it.

First, let's go over the material and tools you'll need to have on hand before you begin. Because it's a soft wood and easily worked I'd make the head out of Bass wood. Get a block of Bass wood 6 x 7 x 10 inches. This will make a dummy's head of professional size. If you can't get a solid block of Bass wood that size, then get as large pieces as you can and glue them together in the size block I designated. You can buy Bass wood at most any lumber yard. The best wood glue I've found is called "Elmer's Glue-All," although any good furniture glue will do. To do the carving you'll need a sharp knife-like instrument such as the "X-acto" blade set which you can buy at any arts supply store. And last you should have a package of both heavy and light sandpaper. Once you have all these prescribed tools and materials you're ready to begin work.

In front of you on your table or work bench you have an oblong block of Bass wood which has to be carved into the roundness of a head with a face on one side of it. A face that has form, features, expression and character. And all these things must be put there by the sharp edge of your carving tool.

Right here I'm going to hang out the warning signals. Stop, Look, and Listen! This is not like making a papier mâché head where you start out with a head of clay which you can mold and re-mold and change and re-change with a flick of your finger tips. This is wood, and the only way you get a feature or an expression on the face is by carving it there. What it will look like—nose, mouth, eyes, everything depends on you. And once you've carved anything on the wood it's pretty permanent. So the great danger in carving is that you may cut off too much wood. Therefore, figure out in advance where and how much you want to carve each little area of the wood surface before you put the knife into it. Even when you know how much you want to take off at any given point don't cut it off in one large piece. Carve it off a little bit at a time. You may find that you didn't need or want as much off as you originally estimated. To protect you against doing that I'd advise that, where ever possible, you take off wood with heavy sandpaper rather than the carving tool. However, if you should happen to cut off a section of the wood by mistake you can glue it back on again, and continue carving. But remember a glued seam is not as permanent as the solid wood. So be careful.

As was the case earlier, in making the clay

head, I can't go into detail in telling you how to sculpture the face in the wood. That would require writing another whole book covering anatomy, art, sculpturing, and many related subjects. The head and face you carve out of the Bass wood will be the result of your own individual artistic ability. But don't let that deter you. Don't say, "Oh, gee, I can't do that!" You'll be surprised what you can do if you try. In all the cities where Jerry and I go, youngsters are always coming to our dressing room to show us dummies they've made themselves. The dummies are all different, but they all have personality and character, and they're all pretty darn good! So don't have any fears about sculpturing the face. You'll find out you can do it. Just carve off the first chip and you'll be on your way.

As I said I can't tell you how to carve the particular face you want for your dummy, because each one of you will probably have a different idea of what you want your dummy to look like. What I can do, briefly, is outline the progression of steps in the carving.

Right now you have that oblong block of Bass wood 6 x 7 x 10 inches. The 10 inches is the height, the 6 inches is the width across the face, and the seven inches is the depth of the head from front to back. The first thing to do is to turn to one of the 7-inch wide sides on the block, and with a pencil draw a profile outline of your dummy's face, head and neck on that surface

(Fig. 9). This is the surface which will eventually be one side of the dummy's head.

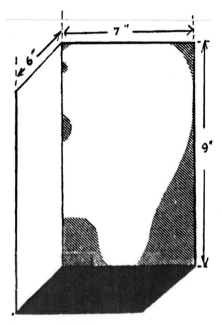

Fig. 9—Draw outline on side of block with pencil.

In making this drawing there are two important points. 1) Don't draw a nose or ears on your profile. Later you'll cut out separate pieces of wood and glue them on where the nose and ears should go. 2) Draw your profile sketch so that it covers as much of the surface of that side of the wood block as possible. This will save your having to do a lot of carving, because many areas on the surface of the block can remain almost intact as surfaces on the head of your dummy. For instance, for the top of the dummy's head you can use some of the top surface of the wood block. On the surface which will be the front of the face you can use some of the flat original surface for the forehead, cheeks and jaw.

Don't get the idea from this that you won't have to do any carving at all on these areas. You'll have to do some, but not as much as you would if you didn't take advantage of them. And don't think that by using all the wood block for your dummy's head that it will be too large. The measurements I gave you, 6 x 7 x 10 inches, is a head size used by most ventriloquists.

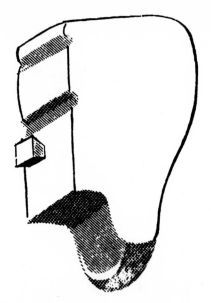

Fig. 10—Saw along pencil lines to cut out profile.

So, once you have drawn the face on the side surface the next job is to cut that profile out of the wood. Take a saw, and saw along the pencil lines you drew. Saw through the entire 6-inch thickness of the block. Saw in for the hairline, in for the eye area, omit the nose, in for the chin, and down to the bottom for the neck. Then starting at the top again saw down over the outline of the back of the head and neck. When you have finished you will see that you have accomplished quite a lot of work. You'll see that with a few strokes of the saw you have cut out what would have taken you many hours to do with a carving tool.

You now have a rather strange looking creature which is slightly square on the sides, but which in the front and back contains the preliminary contour of your dummy's head, face and neck (Fig. 10). Take a look at it in profile. Even now you can see a little bit of your dummy which is to be.

Now look at the face from the front, and with a pencil draw an outline of the face from the head-on view (Fig. 11-a). Then saw along these new pencil lines. When you've finished you'll then have two different facial planes. Even though the head still contains many sharp edges at this point your dummy's head is pretty well shaped for only having done two bits of sawing.

Next cut out a square piece of Bass wood large enough for you to later carve it into a nose. Then glue this piece on the front surface where you want the nose to be. Then cut out two more square pieces of Bass wood large enough to later sculpture into ears and glue them on the side

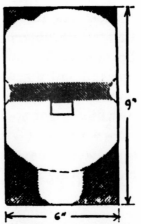

Fig. 11-a—Draw outline of head from head-on view. Saw along pencil outline.

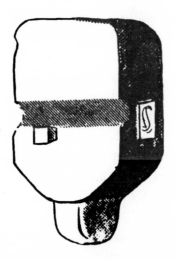

Fig. 11-b—Glue on nose and ear pieces.

surfaces (Fig. 11-b). You can easily locate the

place to put the ears. When looking at the head in profile, the top of the ears are usually at the same height as the top of the eyes, and the bottom of the ears come down to the same distance as the bottom of the nose.

After you've glued on these pieces for the nose and ears the next step is to take this wooden head which is still somewhat square, and begin to make it round (Fig. 12-a). This will have to be done with your carving tool or that heavy sandpaper. You will note in Fig. 12-a that there is a little indentation on the corners of the eye areas. This is just a little depression that goes gradually from the eyes toward the ears. It doesn't go all the way back along the side of the head as the figure might indicate.

After you've done the first preliminary work, such as rounding off the sharp edges, stop. Then take a pencil and draw on the face where you want the various features to be—draw an outline of the eyes, sketch in the eyebrows, indicate the mouth and lips, outline the cheeks, and draw the hair style and the hairline (Fig. 12-b).

Now continue your carving keeping the features in mind. Continue your rounding out of the head, but at the same time remember that the cheeks and hair (as well as the nose and ears) protrude from the surface of the head, while the eyes and the area around the mouth and chin are deep set into the head. With that in mind begin to carve away the wood which will create those features. Do it just a little bit at a time.

At first the head will look as if it's covered with large lumps. But it's from these lumps that you'll

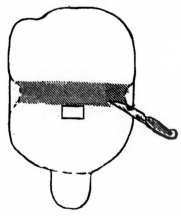

Fig. 12-a—Carve slight depression from eyes to ears.

Fig. 12-b—Draw outline of features to be carved: eyes, mouth, eyebrows, hair and hairline.

carve the features in more detail. So carve away

at those lumps slowly and carefully until they gradually take the shape and size of your dummy's facial characteristics. None of the features has to be too perfect or life-like. You're not sculpturing "Mr. Venus." You're carving a cute perky little dummy. So don't try to carve the various features in fine, minute detail. The ears, for example, don't have to have all the curlicues and lobes that your own ears have. Just suggest them. Another thing, if, after carving you find that the surface is a little rough and contains sharp edges from the strokes of the carving tool, go over it with a piece of fine sandpaper, and you'll bring the surface down to a nice smooth finish.

After you have completely carved the head and are satisfied with the various features, you're still not finished with your work. What you have now is a head of solid wood. What you need is a hollow head into which you can place the mechanism for the moving parts.

So the next task is to cut the head into two halves. You do this with a saw just as you did on the papier mâché head. That is to say, you saw it at an angle just in front of the ears with the ears remaining on the back half. Now you have two halves of solid Bass wood. Enough of this wood now has to be removed to allow you to install the various gadgets which move the mouth and eyes.

With your carving tool or some other gouging instrument begin to scoop out the wood. Continue to scoop it out until each half of the head is down to a shell about one-inch thick. Be careful. Remember each scoopful of wood you take out makes your shell thinner and thinner. And a misdirected stroke might plunge the carving tool right through the face. So just take your time and it will come out all right. Having hollowed out the shells, you're ready now to put in the controls for the mouth and eyes, after which you'll glue the two halves of the head back together again, and your dummy will be just about ready for action.

During your reading of these last several pages, constructing a dummy of your own, whether of wood or papier mâché, may sound to you like a lot of work. I'm not going to say it isn't. But I will say that it isn't too difficult nor too complicated for you to do, and I guarantee that you'll enjoy doing it. As I said in the beginning, your completed dummy will be a part of you and your abilities, and you'll be mighty proud of it.

Mechanism for Realism—Part 1 Moving Mouth

After you have constructed the dummy's head the next problem is to get the mouth to move. No matter whether you made your head out of wood or papier mâché the mechanism for the moving mouth is the same for both. The process of installing this mechanism may be more or less complicated, so I've made some diagrams which I hope will help you if you should get stuck anywhere along the way.

The first thing that has to be done is to cut the mouth and jaw free from the rest of the head. Take a pencil and draw a line straight down from each corner of the mouth, continue each line under the chin and down about a half inch on the neck. Then draw a horizontal line on the neck to connect the two lines you drew down from the corners of the mouth. Be sure these lines coming down are straight (Fig. 13).

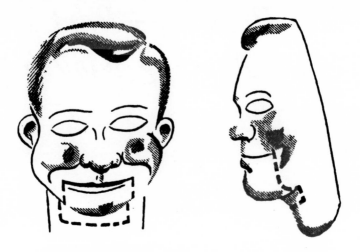

Fig. 13—Cut the jaw and mouth free from the head.

Now with a single-edge razor blade or X-acto blade (for the papier mâché head) or a pointed saw (for the wooden head) cut out the jaw following along the penciled lines you drew. I'd advise that you start on the neck where the horizontal line meets the vertical line coming down from right corner of jaw, and saw or cut upward to the corner of the mouth, across between the lips, then down from the corner of the mouth to the neck again, and across the neck to the point where you started. When you have finished sawing from the mouth to the neck, you can then lift that section of the jaw right out of the head.

Now you must install some kind of a mechanism by which you can make that jaw move up and down to simulate talking. I call this mechanism a "casket" because when it's constructed it has the shape of a little casket. Here are the various items you'll need to build the casket:

MATERIAL

1) A cigar box or small cheese box.
2) Wire brads (to nail cigar or cheese box).
3) Two metal axles (made from coat hanger).
4) Two non-metal washers (into which the axles will fit).
5) Two small screw-eyes.
6) Package of strong tailor pins.
7) Bobby pins or paper clips.
8) Rubber bands or light spring.
9) Three feet of strong LINEN fishing line.

This casket has to be constructed so that it fits into the head of the dummy as part of the mouth. Its size therefore depends on the size of the head you have made. Before you start to build it let me explain what it looks like and its use. This may help you better understand how to construct it. Also study the drawings.

The casket is made out of pieces of the cigar box or cheese box. It has two sides and a top but no bottom. For the front end you use that jaw which you cut out of the head. The back end is a piece of cigar or cheese box. There is also a small piece on the bottom at the front. Through the two sides at the back of the casket there is an axle. The ends of this axle are held to the inside walls of the head with a couple of washers. On top of the casket there is a small screw-eye and another one on the small piece of wood attached to the bottom.

The various parts function in this way. The axle does the dual job of holding the casket in place and at the same time allowing it to rotate freely when the jaw moves up and down. The small screw-eye on the bottom holds one end of the string or cord which pulls the jaw down to open the mouth. (The other end of the string is connected to the trigger on the pole. And of course it's this trigger which you'll use to make your dummy pretend to talk.)

The small screw-eye on the top of the casket holds one end of a rubber band or spring which will automatically pull the mouth closed again each time you release the pressure on the trigger.

There is another and lesser important use for the casket when it is all finished and installed. The top can be painted a reddish color to resemble the interior of the mouth, and a row of little white teeth can be painted on just back of the lower lip.

Now let's get down to the actual constructing of the casket. Its dimensions, as I said, depend on the size of the head you made, and especially the size of the mouth and jaw. Therefore, I can't give you any standard measurement to follow. The head each of you makes will be different. What I can do is indicate some proportional dimensions to be your guide.

The front end of the top of the casket has to be made so that it fits flush against the inside contour of the jaw piece which you have removed. That means you make the top of the casket the same width as the jaw. Likewise the sides of the casket in the front will be as wide as the jaw is long, not including the neck portion. The back end of the casket is simply a piece of the cheese or cigar box long enough to join the two sides. This end doesn't have to fit any contour as the front end does.

The length of the sides and the top of the casket are determined by how far back in the head the axle is going to rest. That, in turn, is determined by the "jaw line." Take your fingers and hold them on both sides of your own face just under and a shade in front of your ears. Now move your jaw up and down. You find that this is the point where your own jaw seems to pivot. Locate where those same two points would be on each side of the dummy's head. There is where the axle must go—between those two points inside the head. Since in cutting the head in half you left the ears on the back portion, this axle will be installed pretty close to the back edge of the front half of the head.

Once you know where the axle is to go, you can then figure out how long to make the sides and top of the casket. Then simply cut pieces of the cigar box wood to the size and shape you need and nail them together (Fig. 14-a). Make

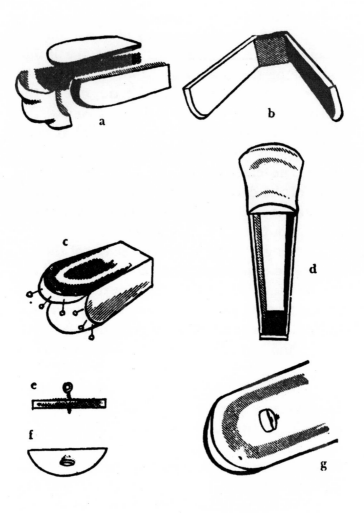

Fig. 14—a. Pieces of casket cut to contour of jaw. b. Sides and back of casket joined. c. Use pins and glue to join casket to jaw. d. Bottom view of casket. e, f. 2 views of the screw-eye in bottom of casket. g. View of screw-eye in top of casket.

the back end piece a little less than the width of

the jaw. The casket will then taper slightly from front to back (Fig. 14-b). Next cut a little 1-inch piece and nail it on the bottom as far front as possible. That completes the casket except for fastening it to the jaw piece. If your head is wood, use small wire brads. If you're working with a papier mâché head, then use strong straight pins like a tailor uses. Push the pins through the front of the papier mâché jaw right into the wood of the casket (Fig. 14-c). You might also glue the casket front to the jaw piece.

Next put in the two screw-eyes. One goes into the little piece of cigar box on the bottom (Fig. 14-e,f), and the other screws in just about center on the top of the casket 1-inch back of the lip. (Fig. 14-g). The moment you get your screw-eye in the bottom attach your three feet of linen fishing line to it. Later it may be awkward to attach.

At this point it's time to install the axle. For the axle you can use a piece of straightened-out coat hanger. Since the axle must go through the sides of the casket, the casket itself should extend back in the head a little beyond the points you've indicated as the jaw-line. So put the jaw and casket back in the head and hold it firmly in place with your hand. Make sure it doesn't move. If you are working with a papier mâché head, the next step is to take the piece of coat hanger which you are using for the axle and push it right through the head from the outside at the point you've designated as the jaw line,

Push it through and out the other side of the head at the point you've marked as the jaw line. If you've connected the two jaw line points correctly the axle should be perfectly horizontal.

Now remove the axle from the head for a minute, and then push it through one side again, and keeping it horizontal, push it against the side of the casket so that it makes a mark. Then remove the axle and casket, and drill a hole in the side of the casket at the mark made by the axle. This hole must be just big enough to let the axle pass through it. Next, put the jaw and casket back in the head again, and push the axle through the head, through the hole in the one side .of the casket, and, keeping it horizontal, press it against the other side of the casket. Again remove the axle and casket, and drill a hole in the other side of the casket where the axle touched. Then put the casket back in the head and push the axle through the head, through both sides of the casket and out the other side of the head. Look at the axle—it must be horizontal. If it is, you're ready to lock it into place.

To do this, pull the axle out of the head again for a moment. Then push it through one side of the head, and before it reaches the casket, slip a fibre washer on it. Then push the axle through the two sides of the casket, slip another washer on it and push the axle through the other side of the head. NOTE: the hole in these fibre washers should be just large enough to fit the axle.

Once you have the axle through the head, glue the washers to the sides of the head and pack plastic wood around them. These washers will give the ends of the axle a place to rest on and also keep the axle from slipping out of line. Now you have the jaw and casket securely in the head, but you still have both ends of your coat hanger axle sticking out of the sides of the head. Simply take a wire shears and snip off the ends as close to the outside of the head as possible.

The foregoing described how to install the casket and axle in the papier mâché head. For the wooden head you follow the same directions except that you can't push the coat hanger axle through the sides of the wooden head. It's too hard and thick. So you'll have to drill two holes in the sides of the head at the jaw line points (Fig. 15).

We have already installed the string which opens the dummy's mouth, so we now need something to pull it closed again. For this we use a rubber band or spring. One end is fastened to the screw-eye on the top of the casket. The other end has to be attached to the top of the inside of the head, by using a bobby pin or paper clip. If you use a paper clip first straighten it out into a long "U" shape. The bobby pin is already made in that shape. Then push the two pointed ends through the top of the head from the inside, at a point directly over the screw-eye on the top of the casket (Fig. 15).

Now you have the two pointed ends of the pin

or clip sticking through the top of the head. Bend these ends in half until they point back down and then push them right back into the head again. This is done not only to get rid of these pointed ends sticking up through the head, but it also anchors the clip or pin firmly into the head. Whatever pull the rubber band or spring now exerts on the loop end of the clip, it will also be pulling the ends in tighter and thus the clip or pin can't come out.

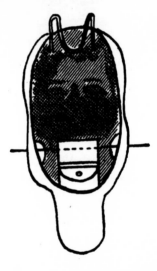

Fig. 15—Install axle and rubber band holder.

When this is done stretch the rubber band or spring between the screw-eye on the casket and the clip on the head. Now you should be able to pull the jaw down with your hand and have it snap shut by itself. If you find that the jaw sticks a little or moves slowly it may be because of some bit of wood or papier mâché inside the head. Carve or sandpaper these points until the jaw moves up and down as freely as it should.

You've got the mouth so it will close, now you have to get it to open. For that you use the string which you attached to the screw eye on the bottom of the casket. Let's have a look at the route it takes, and perhaps that will help you install it. From the screw-eye, the string goes back and down through the neck to the top of the pole; through the top of the pole and out of the pole again at a point a half inch below the neck and is finally fastened to the trigger (Fig. 16-a).

You can see from this that before you can install either the string or the pole, you first have to drill a hole in the pole. This hole should be about a quarter-inch in diameter. Pick out a spot on the top surface of the pole and as far back as possible. Now drill a hole down at such an angle that the other end of it will be on the front of the pole about a half inch below the neck (Fig. 16-b). Take sandpaper and smooth off the edges of the hole at each end. This will prevent the edges from rubbing and wearing the string which would eventually break.

Now thread the string through the pole. I call it string, but as you recall I advised you to get linen fishing line. Don't get nylon because it will stretch. And if it stretches too much when you press on the trigger the mouth may not open.

At the same time as you drill the hole for the fishline to go through, I want you to do something else. At the top of the pole, on the side

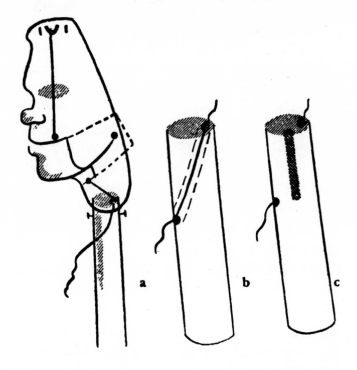

Fig. 16—a. Route taken by string from mouth through the pole. b. Drill hole in pole for string. c. Make trough for eyes string (Chap. 7).

where your thumb is, dig a little trough about a quarter of an inch deep. Dig it from the top of the pole down to about a half inch below the neck. This trough has nothing to do with the moving mouth mechanism, but you will need it later if you install moving eyes (Fig. 16c). Digging this trough now will make it easier and less complicated than doing it after the pole has been permanently installed.

Speaking of using the fishing line for the string reminds me of the time I played in Milwaukee. The dressing rooms overlooked the river. In fact the other acts on the bill used to drop a line out their window and fish. One day I decided I'd try it, but I didn't have any fishing tackle. Then I remembered Jerry. So I took the string out of him and made a hook out of a safety pin and dropped it down into the river. Believe it or not, I caught a fish! Jerry says there's something very fishy about that story!

The main thing lacking on the head now is the pole. Push the pole up in the neck of the dummy up to a point where it will be secure, but not interfere with the casket mechanism. When you've located that point, glue the pole to the neck, and then fill the hollow between the poles and sides of the neck with plastic wood (Fig. 17-a). When this hardens the pole will be securely in place. Now try the string. Pull it and the mouth should open. Let go and the rubber band or spring should snap it shut again.

You now need the trigger to which you attach this loose end of the fishing line. Cut a piece of wood from your cigar or cheese box about 2 inches long and 1/4-inch wide. About a half inch from one end of this piece bore a hole large enough for the "string" to go through. This is your trigger. Taper the back end of the trigger slightly. On the pole, about 1 inch down from where the string comes out of the pole, carve a little trough about a half-inch deep, an inch and a half long, and wide enough for the trigger to fit in. Put the trigger in the center of this trough and drive an axle through the pole so that it enters the trough, passes through the trigger and

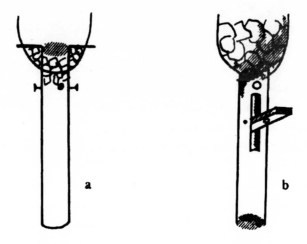

Fig. 17—a. Attach pole to neck with Plastic Wood. b. Install trigger.

into the pole again at the other side of the trough (Fig. 17-b). A wire brad might well do as your axle. Now, keeping the trigger horizontal, pull the string as taut as you can without having it pull the mouth open. Then tie it through the hole in the trigger as securely as you are able to.

When you have done this, you have now completely installed all the mechanism for making the mouth open and close (Fig. 18). Pick up the

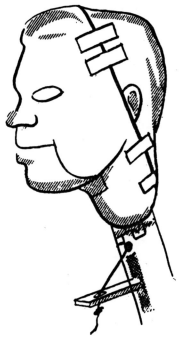

Fig. 18—Head with complete mouth moving mechanism.

pole, put your finger on the trigger, and press and release it. The mouth opens and closes. At last you've finally got those other lips which will move to create the ventriloquial illusion.

All that remains to be done now is to close up the head and paint it. And that is quite simple. Closing the head is just a matter of putting the two halves of the head together. If your head is made of wood, glue the halves together with that strong glue. If the head is papier mâché you put the two halves together with more papier mâché. Using the paperhanger's paste and the paper towels, as you did originally, make up a new batch of papier mâché. Holding the two halves of the head together, put these little pieces of papier mâché along the entire seam made by the two halves. Only this time, before putting the pieces of paper on, wring them out thoroughly. Remember to let them overlap, and use plenty of paste, and put on two layers. When this dries, your dummy's head will finally all be in one piece again. If this patchwork along the seam is rough or bumpy sandpaper the papier mâché very lightly. And with this the construction of your dummy's head is fully completed, except for one last thing. Put your hand on the pole and your finger on the trigger in the manner you wish to use it. Then mark off the pole about an inch down from your hand, and saw off the pole at that line. This ends any nailing, sawing or carving on the dummy's head. It's done.

Mechanism for Realism—Part 2 Moving Eyes

Now that you've constructed the moving mouth and closed up the head again, this will probably seem a little late for me to bring up the matter of installing moving eyes in your dummy. However, I delayed it purposely, because it isn't absolutely necessary for you to concern yourself with moving eyes right in the beginning. You can learn all the basic steps of ventriloquism and go out and entertain successfully without your dummy ever rolling his eyes. Moving the eyes is just one more manipulation for you to think about, and you're going to have enough things to concentrate on in the early stages as it is. So I'd recommend that you build your dummy with eyes that don't move and install the moving eyes at a later date after you've mastered the other more essential problems.

But regardless of when you install the eyes that move, the material and construction remain the same. This is true whether your dummy's head is made of wood or papier mâché. So, first here's the list of supplies you'll need to build the mechanism for moving eyes.

MATERIAL

1.) Two wooden balls one inch in diameter
2.) Two 1½-inch "L" screws.
3.) Two metal threaded rods one-fourth inch in diameter, and four inches long.
4.) Eight nuts to fit the threaded rods.
5.) Plastic wood (which you already have).
6.) A strip of hard wood or metal a half inch wide and about three inches long, ⅛-inch thick.
7.) Two screw eyes.
8.) One rubber band or a fine delicate spring.
9.) Three feet of plastic tubing (such as is used in goldfish tanks).
10.) Three feet of fishline. (You may have some left over after installing the moving mouth.)

Obviously, to install the mechanism for the moving eyes the dummy's head must be open so you can work from the inside. If you decide to put the eyes in at the same time as you do the moving mouth your dummy's head will already be open. If you do it at a later time, as I suggested, you'll have to saw the head into two halves again. In the latter case the important thing to remember is that you must saw open the head through the seam made when you put the two halves together originally.

If you made your dummy's head of papier mâché you covered the seam with more papier mâché; if the head is wood you glued the seam together. In either case the area along this seam is naturally the weakest part of the head. So, in re-opening the head if you saw through in some other part you'll then have two weak seams, which might lead to your dummy's head splitting open sometime in the future.

So find that seam around the head and in front of the ears where you first put the two halves together, and saw through until you have the head in two parts once again. When this is done, the next step is to cut out the section you've indicated on the dummy's face for the eyes. Cut out that part which would be the eye-ball; that is, the oval-shaped area between the upper and lower lids. Don't saw or cut away the eye-lids.

Once you have cut out the two eye holes you're ready to begin work on constructing the mechanism for moving the eyes. The first item of material you were to get was two wooden balls at least one inch in diameter, depending on the size of the eye openings. These will become your dummy's eye-balls. If you can't buy them in a hardware store you may try to get these two balls made for you at a lumber yard. But there is one other place where you might find them already made for you—among your toys. There are all kinds of children's bowling games which contain small wooden balls of the size you need. If you don't have any games at home which ʼare equipped with balls you can probably buy a game at the 5 & 10 cent store. Also you might get a doll made of balls at an infant shop.

Your next job is to put one of those metal threaded rods through the center of each of the wooden balls. So, drill a hole vertically thru the center of each ball (Fig. 19). Let me warn

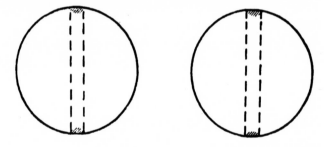

Fig. 19—Drill a hole through the dead center of the wooden balls.

you that the holes must be drilled down the dead center of each ball or else they won't rotate correctly. If they're off-center even the slightest bit you'll find that they'll rotate in a wobbly fashion and may even stick against the inside of the head.

After you've drilled the holes, take one of the

balls and put one of the threaded rods through it. Then screw on two nuts on each end of the rod, top and bottom (Fig. 20). On the top screw

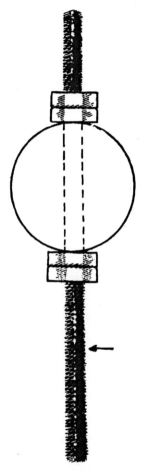

Fig. 20—Threaded rod is installed through the wooden ball, the nuts are locked in place, and the excess rod is sawed off.

the two nuts down about an inch on the rod and

then lock them. You lock the two nuts together by taking your wrench or pliers and twisting each of them in opposite directions. Once the two top nuts are locked in place, screw the two bottom nuts up to a point where they touch the wooden ball very lightly which is already up against the two locked nuts on the top. Spin the ball with your hand and see if it turns quickly and easily and is not retarded by any of the nuts. If it's okay then lock the two bottom nuts at that point in the same way as the two on the top.

Now you'll find that much more of the threaded rod extends beyond the two bottom nuts than the one inch which you left at the top. If this doesn't interfere with the casket, or if it doesn't show when the mouth is open, leave it àlone. If it does, then cut off as much as is necessary so that it won't. When you have completed this work with one ball, follow each of the exact same steps with the other ball and rod.

The "L" screws are put in next. The threaded rods were inserted vertically through the exact center, or diameter, of each wooden ball. The "L" screws, on the other hand, must be inserted through the exact horizontal center on the line which would be the circumference of each ball. When you have found this point mark it with a small "x" in pencil (Fig. 21). Then take the two "L" screws and roughen up the top part of the "L" with a file. After you've done that screw in each "L" screw at the points you marked with the "x" on each wooden ball. Screw them in until they are half way through the ball, and make sure when you stop that the top of the "L" screws are in a vertical position from top to bottom.

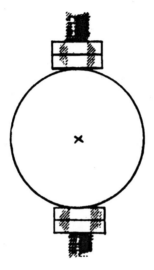

Fig. 21—Mark spot where "L" screw is to go.

You're ready now to mount the two wooden balls inside the head to act as the moving eyes. So, from inside the head, hold each ball against the cut-out eye holes in the dummy's face. Then turn each ball so that both the "L" screws are directly in the center of the ball facing back toward the interior of the head. Holding each ball so that it won't move, draw an eye on each with a pencil. You naturally do this from outside the face. Don't do any more than the pencil sketch of the eye at this time. You can paint the eyes after they've been installed (Fig. 22).

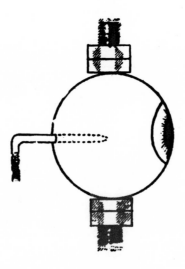

Fig. 22—The eye is now ready for mounting into your
dummy's head.

Now get out your can of plastic wood. Take
each ball, one at a time, and put it in position
behind the cut-out eye hole with the threaded
rod in a vertical line. Then, holding the face
down, start to pack mounds of plastic wood on
and around both ends of the rod to attach them
to the inside of the head (Fig. 23). Pile the
plastic wood up to and over the two locked nuts
but make sure it doesn't touch the wooden ball.
Also, be sure the balls are not flush against the
eye-holes. They must be as close to the eye-holes
as possible and still not touch them. If they do
the eyes won't move freely. So when you've
packed in the plastic wood gently turn the balls
to see that they still rotate in an easy motion. If

they do, you've installed them correctly. Then set the head face down and allow it to dry thoroughly. When the plastic wood hardens the threaded rods will be firmly attached to the inside of the head.

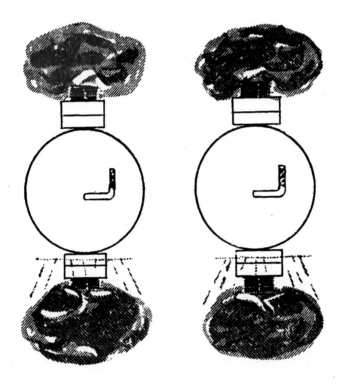

Fig. 23—Pack plastic wood around both ends of the rod and attach them to the inside of the head.

You've got the eyes installed. The next job is to get them to move back and forth together. Right now one eye could easily move to the right while the other moves to the left, and vice

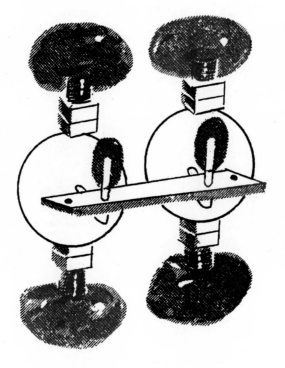

Fig. 24—Place the strip of metal or wood on the "L" screws, so that both eyes move together.

versa. You've got to get their movements synchronized. This is easily done. After the mounds of plastic wood, which hold the eyes in place, have thoroughly dried and hardened, center the two "L" screws again facing toward the back of the head. To do this center the eyeballs from the front. Once they're centered, hold them securely with your fingers, and measure the distance between the two "L" screws. Then take that three-inch strip of hard wood or metal and measure that distance on it. Then at each of these points on the strip bore a hole just large enough to fit down over each "L" screw. At the same time bore a hole of the same size about $\frac{1}{4}$ inch in from each end of the strip. When the holes are made slip the strip down over the two "L" screws (Fig. 24). Now by holding the strip with your fingers and moving it back and forth you will see that the two wooden balls rotate the same distance right or left together. In other words that little strip of wood or metal brings the two balls into synchronization and makes them rotate together in either direction. So that the strip won't come off the "L" screws pack a little plastic wood around the top part of the "L."

While you now have the wooden balls, or eyes, so that they'll move back and forth, you still have to install some means of finger tip control which will work after you've put the two halves of the head back together. To do this, start out by putting a mound of plastic wood on each side of the interior of the head in a line with the "L" screws. Then sink a screw-eye (like the ones you used in the casket) into each of these mounds of plastic wood. Sink them deep enough so that only about half the rounded screw-eyes stick out of the plastic wood. Let this harden until it holds the screw-eyes in securely (Fig. 25).

Once you have these screw-eyes firmly installed in the sides of the head the next pieces of equipment you work with are a rubber band or a spring and a couple feet of fishline (the same as you used in constructing the moving jaw). Tie the rubber band or connect the spring between the screw-eye on the right side of the head and the hole you made in the right end of the wood or metal strip (Fig. 25). Be sure the rubber band is taut enough so that it pulls the eye unit to the right of the inside of the head. This action makes the dummy's eyeballs look to the left. Move the strip to the left with your fingers, and then release it. The rubber band or spring should pull the eye unit back to the right again.

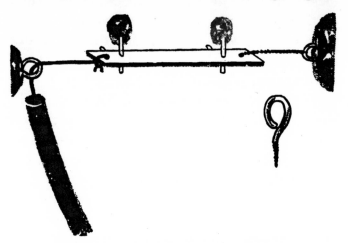

Fig. 25—The assembly of the eye mechanism.

I have used both rubber bands and springs in my dummies and find they both work equally well. But, neither the rubber band nor the spring is going to last forever. From time to time both will lose their elasticity and will have to be replaced. The spring, being metal, will last longer than the rubber band.

When the rubber band or spring is installed your dummy's eye unit is pulled to the right and he's looking left at you. And that's where they will always look except at such times as you pull the eyes to the center or to the right. You naturally want your dummy to look in all directions so you must now install the last bit of mechanism which will enable the dummy to do just that. Take a couple feet of the fishline and tie one end of it tightly around the hole you bored in the left end of the wood or metal strip. (Fig. 25). Then thread it through the screw-eye on the left side of the head. Next take a couple feet of the plastic tubing which you bought at the pet shop and chalking the fishline thoroughly, feed it down through the tubing (Fig. 25). At this point stop and take a trial run. Pull on the fishline. The eyes should move to the right. Release the line and the rubber band or spring should pull them back to the left again.

If the eyes are working back and forth in the right manner then put the top of the plastic tubing against the inside wall of the head and fasten it there with plastic wood. Pile the plastic wood around it generously, and when it hardens the tubing will be held firmly in place.

The tubing with the fishline inside of it now has to go down through the pole. This is why you earlier made the trough on the thumb side of the pole which you haven't used yet. Feed the plastic tubing down through that trough and it should come out of the pole about two inches above your thumb. Cut off the plastic tubing (but not the fishline inside of it) about an inch after it comes out of the pole. You can pack plastic wood around the tubing to keep it in the trough.

Now construct another trigger on the pole for your thumb to control. Build this trigger exactly as you did the one for controlling the dummy's mouth. When you've done that pull the fishline taut, but yet it doesn't move the eyes, and tie it to the hole in the trigger. Be sure the trigger is perfectly horizontal when you tie the fishline to it. With this your dummy should have moving eyes (Fig. 26). Try it. Press the trigger with your thumb. The eyes should now be looking away from you. Release the trigger and the eyes should be looking at you. Pull the trigger half way down and the dummy should be looking straight ahead. If you forget about the trigger momentarily the dummy will be looking at you which is natural.

Let me remind you at this point that if you are left handed you should reverse the entire procedure of installing the eye control system. The rubber band or spring should go on the left and the fishline and tubing on the right.

If the eyes are working to your satisfaction there is only one thing remaining to do, and that is to put the two halves of the head together as I described in Part 1 of this chapter. When you close up the head all the machinery for the mov-

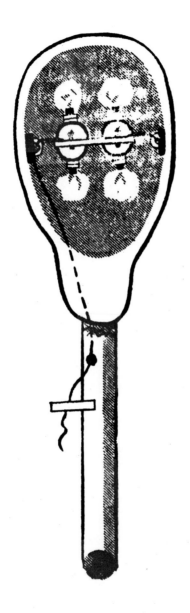

Fig. 26—Completed eye mechanism.

ing parts has been installed and almost all the work on your dummy's head is completed.

Painting the Dummy and Building the Body

Having installed a moving mouth your dummy at last has movement and animation. It needs one more thing to really bring it to life— color. In other words it has to be painted. Here is the material you'll need:

MATERIAL

1) A jar of white poster paint.
2) A jar of burnt sienna poster paint.
3) One half-inch wide paint brush for broad work.
4) One narrow paint brush for fine detail work.

Before you do any painting, first draw with a

pencil the outline of the lips, eyebrows, eyes, and the hairline. Then, except for these areas, give the entire face and neck a coat of "flesh" color. To get a flesh color mix one part burnt sienna with ten parts of white, plus a little dash of water. This should turn out to be a good flesh tone. And when you're mixing this paint, be sure to mix enough to complete the job. If you happen to run out of paint when you're only half finished it might be difficult to mix up a second lot that will exactly match the original shade. Also, later on, you'll have to paint the hands the same color. So make up a lot of this flesh color. Put a coat of this shade over the entire head except for the areas you've outlined. This is all poster paint I'm describing which is good for papier mâché, but for a more lasting finish on a wood head use oil paint.

For the hair use any shade you want which will contrast with the flesh color. If you want the hair real dark use nothing but burnt sienna. For lighter shades just add more white until you get the desired color. Then paint on the hair following the hair line you pencilled on the head. For the eyebrows and the outline of the eyes you may use burnt sienna. Even if your hair is light, I'd advise that you use straight burnt sienna for the brows.

The cheeks and the lips must also contrast with the over-all flesh color of the dummy. So for the cheeks add one part more of burnt sienna to a small portion of mixture you already made.

For the lips add two more parts burnt sienna to that mixture.

I've left the eyes to the last because they require more detailed work than the rest of the painting. It might be best to first pencil in a round pupil in the center of the eyeball you've drawn.

Paint the eyes from the outside in. Paint the iris a little lighter shade than the pupil. The pupil itself should be straight burnt sienna. Then outline the entire iris with a ring of solid burnt sienna. The rest of the eyeball paint white. Remember the darker the shade of the eyes, the more effective they are. While we're on the subject of the eyes, I might add that the painting of the eyebrows is highly important. You can paint them any size and shape you desire, but just remember it's from the area around the eyes that we get a lot of the dummy's facial expression, and thus some of his character. So in painting the brows take the dummy's personality into consideration.

If you recall my describing the uses of the casket, I said that the top could be painted to resemble the interior of the mouth. So with the white paint, paint a little row of white teeth just back of the lower lip in the shape of a horseshoe. Behind the teeth paint the top of the casket a full shade of burnt sienna.

Right here, you can stop and take a long look at your dummy's head. It may seem like a long time since you started to build it, but at last it's done, painted and ready for use. Of course the body is still missing, but you can start to use the head in practicing voice and lip control and synchronization in front of the mirror without the body. Meanwhile I'll tell you how to build the body and you can be working on it in your spare moments.

The material you'll have to buy to make the body is as follows:

MATERIAL

1) Two pieces of wood one inch thick, three and a half inches wide and eleven inches long.
2) Two pieces of wood a half inch thick, two and a half inches wide and nine inches long.
3) Four wire coat hangers.
4) A roll of adhesive or electrician's tape.
5) Two pair of child-size long stockings.
6) A pair of child-size gloves.
7) Two feet of wire pliable enough to bend.
8) Whatever costume you desire for the dummy. If it's a boy—a suit, shirt, tie and shoes, or a sweater. If it's a girl—shoes, dress or sweater and skirt.

The over-all size of the body you make will depend on the size of the head you've made. It should be in proportion. You don't want a giant body for a small head, nor a tiny body for a large head. I'd say the average body would be about eleven inches wide across the shoulders and about eleven inches long (without the legs). As I say it will vary according to the size of the dummy's head.

Regardless of size, the shape of the body will be slightly square. You start by making a four-sided frame. When you've decided on the length and width you want, cut your two 1-inch thick pieces of wood for the shoulder section and the seat section, and cut your two half-inch pieces for the sides of the body. This will give you a body that goes straight down from the shoulders to the hips. If you want it to taper in a little at the waist, as you yourself do, then cut the seat section about three inches shorter than the shoulder section.

Before nailing the four pieces together into a frame there are two important things you have to do. First you have to bevel the edges of the shoulder piece (Fig. 27). You can do this either with a saw, plane, file or sandpaper. The main thing is to do it. Since the pole has to go through this shoulder piece you'll have to make a hole through it. Cut this hole in the center of the wood, make it round, and make it 2 inches in diameter. After you've cut this hole take your carving tool and sandpaper again and round off the top edge of the hole. What you're really doing is making a ball-and-socket joint (Fig. 28). In constructing the head I told you the under part of the neck should be "as round as a ball" as it was possible for you to make it. This was because the neck is going to have to sit and maneuver in this hole in the shoulder. Therefore, the rounder and smoother you can make the edge of this hole the easier it will be for you to manipulate the head. The freer it works, the more animation you can give the dummy.

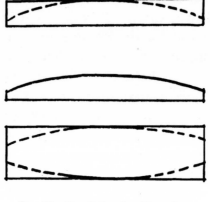

Fig. 27—Bevel the shoulder piece.

Fig. 28—Make hole in center of shoulder section 2″ in diameter.

Once the shoulder piece is finished, then nail on the two sides and the bottom. You will note that the shoulder section and the seat section are 3½ inches wide whereas the side sections are only 2½ inches wide. Thus the shoulder and seat sections will have to be tapered gradually to fit the sides. You now have a framework for the body. Next take the four wire coat hangers and straighten them out (Fig. 29). These hangers are

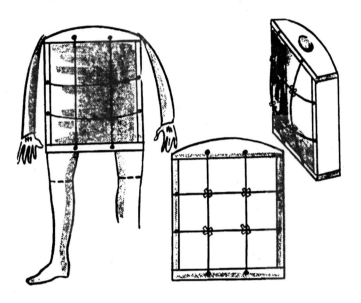

Fig. 29—Construct the framework for the body.

to be fastened to the front of the frame to give it a bowed or bulging effect to look like the chest and ribs. To do this, cut two of the hangers slightly longer than the length of the frame. Then with a pliers, bend the ends of each hanger into a loop, and then fasten them to the shoulder and seat boards with several staples, so that they bulge a little. They should also be attached so that they trisect the top and bottom of the frame. For instance, if the shoulder is twelve inches across, one hanger should be nailed four inches from one end and the other four inches from the opposite end. On the bottom or seat piece they should be nailed in proportional dimensions (Fig. 29).

Then take two more hangers and in the same way bow them horizontally across the frame from side to side and fasten them securely (Fig. 29). You now have two vertical and two horizontal coat hangers criss-crossing each other in a slight bulge. Where the hangers cross each other tape them together with good strong tape. I listed adhesive and electrician's tape. Either one will do the job. This taping keeps the hangers in place as well as strengthening the chest. That finishes the framework for the body except for attaching the arms and legs.

For the legs you simply take a pair of child-size stockings and stuff them. If you have cotton batting, fine. If not, stuffing them with old newspapers will work just as well. Be sure to pack the stuffing down until it's firm and solid. Each leg has to be stuffed in two sections. Stuff the stocking from the toe up to where you want the knee to be. (This is not where the actual knee of the stocking would be.) At this point, pull the stocking together flat and sew a seam all the way across. This seam gives the dummy's leg the kneebend it needs. Continue to stuff the stocking from this seam up to about an inch from the top. Flatten it out and sew another seam across it. This leaves an extra little flap of unstuffed stocking at the top. This is used to attach the leg to the framework of the body. Just tack it on underneath the bottom or seat of the frame. Four or five tacks should do the job. Make and attach a second leg in this same way (Fig. 30).

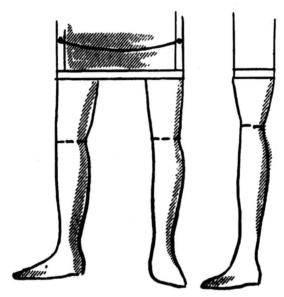

Fig. 30—Attach the legs to the framework.

For the arms you use another pair of child's stockings and a pair of child's gloves. First insert a piece of wire down in each finger and thumb. These pieces of wire should extend well back into the wrist part of the gloves. Then stuff the gloves getting the stuffing down to the ends of the fingers and around the wire. The wire is put in so that you can bend the fingers in the position you want. Without the wire the fingers are going to be straight and wide apart. When a person's hand hangs loosely at the side it is usually slightly cupped with the fingers together. With the wire in the dummy's hands you can make it cupped also. Furthermore, if you ever want the dummy to hold something in his hand, you can bend the fingers around the object and they'll stay in that position.

The gloves make the hands and the stockings make the arms. So, next cut off the feet from the pair of stockings at about ankle height. In place of the feet sew on the two stuffed gloves. Then stuff the stockings solidly up as high as you desire the length of the arms to be. Roughly, the arms should be long enough so that at full length the hands come just a bit below the bottom of the body frame. When you have the desired length for the arms, flatten out the stockings, fold over the top, and tack to the shoulder.

And this should be good news! You can now put away all your tools, and clay, and wood, and glue. Your dummy is finished. Except for dressing it, your manual labor is done. I'll discuss the costuming in full a bit later, but if it's a boy dummy he can wear anything from blue jeans, sweater and sneakers to a full dress suit. Or if it's a girl dummy she can wear an evening gown with rhinestone slippers down to a sweater and skirt. Whatever your dummy wears remember you have to make a slit down the back of the material so you can get your hand in to hold the pole and manipulate the head and mouth.

You're now ready to put the dummy on your knee and take up the advanced work in synchronization of voice and lips. Before that let me tell you about the first dummy I ever made. I had studied Art in school so I didn't have too much trouble carving the head and face. But when it came to the body that was a different matter. I wasn't any carpenter, and I didn't have any instructions such as I've tried to give you in this book; so I didn't know how to build the body. Then I got a bright idea. I went down to a junk dealer and bought an old life-size plaster mannikin that had once displayed the latest fashions in some store window. The head and the face were all cracked and battered, but I didn't need that. All I wanted was the body. So with one "whack" I knocked the head off right at the shoulders. I put in the head I had made and I had a body. There was only one trouble with it—the hole in the shoulders was too big. And every now and then when the dummy was supposed to be talking his head would disappear down inside of the body. So, I decided then and there that I'd better learn how to construct a body.

Lightning Source UK Ltd.
Milton Keynes UK
UKOW042142201112

202509UK00002B/5/P